Frank Lloyd Wright:
21 Surprising Stories

by
Meegan M. Thompson

Table of Contents

Introduction:

In my work at Frank Lloyd Wright's birthplace of Richland Center, Wisconsin, I have heard the whispers and rumors about a man who, while known for his creativity and architecture, had a mysterious and scandalous past. I began to wonder how much of what I hear is based on true facts or embellished, or like a game of telephone where a story is told over and over so it's completely different at the end than what was told at the beginning. In writing this book, I have found that all of the above come into play in the historical figure of Frank Lloyd Wright.

It is easy to picture Wright as a sort of mythic figure. The most widely-seen photographs of the man are from his older years, in which he strikes an astute pose, reinforcing the common image of him as a worldly creative and a famously quirky professional. It is easy to forget that he was actually once a child and then a young man, with a personal life outside his profession. He made his own mistakes and had his own embarrassing secrets, just like everyone else.

Richland Center is a small conservative rural community in Southwest Wisconsin. Scandals were not the norm. Those connected with the few that did occur suffered for years as the residents have a long memory. In the local community, Frank Lloyd Wright seems to be the man you love to hate.

We expect that everyone will learn something new from this book. The facts and stories within are interesting, sometimes scandalous and humorous. Many well-known professionals had checkered pasts while achieving tremendous fame and are worthy of celebration and promotion. It is important to remember both versions of Wright – the mysterious artist and the acclaimed architect – and the community can benefit and profit from the promotion of the man, who was both visionary and human. No other community can claim that they are the birth place of Frank Lloyd Wright or has the only warehouse designed by Frank Lloyd Wright. This fact has been kept a secret for far too long because of the whispers, rumors, and infamous past of Frank Lloyd Wright that many local Richland Center residents are not willing to forget.

The history of the circumstances and choices that led to the character of the man and his path to success adds to the stories being told and encourages more visibility of Richland Center as his birthplace. There is a bit of excitement when you learn something new and you can't wait to share it with others. We hope that sharing some of the peculiar facts will shake things up a bit and make the topic a bit more interesting and entertaining. We hope that others will share our story about Frank Lloyd Wright, his connection to Richland Center and the community project to protect and restore the Frank Lloyd Wright designed warehouse in his hometown.

More information can be found about Richland Center and the restoration project by visiting www.HometownWright.com. Please visit www.FrankLloydWrightStories.com for a series of behind the scenes videos.

Can you imagine what we would know about Frank Lloyd Wright if he were alive during the social media era such as Facebook, Twitter and YouTube?

Thanks for reading and enjoy the book!

Meegan M. Thompson

1. Not only did he never attend school for architecture, he may have never graduated high school

While Wright was thoughtful from childhood and a voracious reader, he was apparently never inspired by structured academia. Theorists suggest that his lack of enthusiasm for formal schooling was due to his parents moving frequently in his childhood, up heaving his scholastic routines. During an economic depression in the 1870s, the Wrights were forced to travel in search of work, moving from Wisconsin to Iowa to Rhode Island to Massachusetts.

Though there is record of his attending a high school in Madison, evidence of his academic performance suggests that he was an average student. His grades varied erratically – records show a good grade in physics, a failing grade in algebra, average grades in rhetoric and botany, etc. There is no evidence of his graduation. He attended the University of Wisconsin at Madison as a special student (the special status further suggests that he was not a high school graduate).

During his time as a student at U-Wisconsin, he worked as a part-time assistant for Allan D. Conover, a civil engineer and professor of engineering at the University. Though his position with Conover was entry-level, Wright's attitude toward academics later in life would suggest he considered his time with Conover a much more worthwhile education than the one he received at the university. Years later, when his son Lloyd was in school, Wright encouraged him to drop out and join him as an apprentice in Europe, arguing that the experience there would be much more valuable than a degree.

Wright's semesters at U-Wisconsin would be the last time the architect dabbled in formal schooling.

2. He turned down an opportunity to formally study architecture in Paris and Rome on a benefactor's dime

The École des Beaux-Arts was (and is) the name of a number of highly influential art schools in France, the most renowned of which is in Paris and is called the École nationale supérieure des Beaux-Arts. A degree from this school would essentially guarantee an exceptional career for the graduate. Famous artists to train there include preeminent Neoclassicist Jacques-Louis David, Claude Monet, and the revolutionary modern artist Henri Matisse. Summarily, the school has educated some of the most innovative and visionary artists of the last four hundred years.

Shortly after the turn of the 20th century, Wright himself had the chance to attend.   Daniel Burnham, a distinguished Chicago architect who was the driving force behind the famous White City in the 1893 world's fair in Chicago, watched Wright's career develop with interest. The two had several mutual social and business connections, and one evening Wright, along with his wife, Catharine, was invited to a dinner at the home of Edward C. Waller. Waller was an important longtime patron of Wright's and a mutual acquaintance of Burnham.

Following dinner, the host ushered Wright and Burnham into a room to have a private conversation over cigars. In short, Burnham offered to send Wright to the École des Beaux-Arts in Paris for a three-year program in architecture, then on to the American Academy in Rome for two years. As Wright spent this five years gaining a formal education in architecture, Burnham would take care of all of Wright's financial expenses, including those of his wife and family. Upon Wright's return, he would have a partnership at Burnham's firm waiting for him.

Such an offer would astound anyone, not only in its promise of a prestigious career and a secure future, but of the implication of the confidence these powerful and respected men had in him. Wright, however, felt the classical training he would receive at these schools would be counterproductive to his goals to create innovative work. He turned the offer down.

Of his decision, he would later write, "I saw myself influential, prosperous, safe with Daniel H. Burnham's power behind me... I felt like an ingrate. Never was the ego within me more hateful than at that moment. But it stood straight up against the very roof of my mind... I'd rather be free and a failure."

Thus, Wright stood firmly in his principles, though he noted that he did not tell his wife what he had declined until some time later.

3. He was a self-made man in multiple senses of the word

Because he did briefly attend college, it may not be accurate to designate him a self-made man. Wright, however, was virtually self-educated in addition to having a talent for self-invention and reinvention, an aptitude that calls for a degree of recognition. That is, he carefully crafted and maintained an image for himself that he felt would increase his standing in the art and architectural world.

While seemingly unimpressed with academic life at the University of Wisconsin-Madison, he was quick to join a fraternity, Phi Delta Theta, and expand his social knowledge. He must have found this access to a higher social stratum invaluable, because he made many sacrifices in order to pay for dues and entertainment. Borrowing money wherever he could, he also pawned prized belongings, like a Swiss gold watch. His mother even pitched in to help him dress the part of a sophisticated artist by sewing her cherished mink collar to his overcoat. Ever occupied with visual effect, Wright adapted trends of dress and eventually developed his own style while at university, walking with a cane while donning a cape and beret or porkpie hat.

His interest in the social scene over the academic community may have served him well in the end. Wright's charm and familiarity with the ways of high society possibly did more to service his career than any formal education would have. Throughout his career, he often had trouble managing his finances, and friendships with various well-to-do patrons of the arts eased his financial stress. His ability to project confidence in himself and his work would also impress clients and benefactors alike.

Again, this confidence came from his extensive social development and fed his talent for self-invention. While this talent is impressive, it does make researching facts about the man rather difficult. For example, he was born in either 1867 or 1869, depending on the source. According to public record, his birth year is 1867; later, however, he would claim to have been born in 1869.

His liberal interpretation of facts is part of the reason that...

4. We know less about him than we should

Considering Wright lived fairly recently, one would think we would know most of the details of his life. In reality, many facts about his life and career are either unknown or confused by widespread conflicting information.

Even his birth name is subject for debate. Some sources say he was born Frank Lincoln Wright, later changing his middle name to honor his maternal family, the Lloyd Joneses. Other sources say he changed his middle name from Lloyd to Lincoln in honor of President Lincoln, later changing it back.

We know for sure that Wright's father was a Baptist preacher named William. His mother was a schoolteacher named Anna. He grew up primarily in Wisconsin. Beyond this, much of his childhood is left up to conjecture.

Wright's parents divorced when he was 18 (according to court records, the proceedings took place in 1885; some sources claim Wright was 16, and still others say he was 14). The reasons for the split are difficult to sort out. Wright would claim throughout his life and in his own autobiography (simply titled, Frank Lloyd

Wright: An Autobiography) that his father abandoned his mother and the rest of the family. Court records tell a different story. Supposedly, as the marriage aged, Anna began to deny William domestic and conjugal services, choosing to focus on rearing her children, particularly her son, Frank Lloyd Wright himself.

Anna's devotion to her son was apparent from the moment of his birth and would remain so throughout her life. Whether or not this contributed to the rift in the Wrights' marriage, it seems that after the divorce, Wright never had further contact with his father and even neglected to attend his funeral (though he would later visit William's grave alone).

Some of the world's most compelling artists have been described as walking contradictions. In a sense, Wright was as well – someone who had a complex view of his world and where he stood within it. His beliefs and observations were often superficially contradictory; his pursuit of truth was convoluted. While this makes for fascinating study of a life, it is also problematic for those who seek to nail down facts about our architect's history and motivation.

5. He is the Father of Organic Architecture, inspired by 19th century Transcendentalists

Wright's idea that a building should emerge out of its natural surroundings was inspired by New England transcendentalists like Ralph Waldo Emerson, as well as by the architect's childhood years spent on an uncle's Wisconsin farm.

As a boy, Wright was rather small and solitary. His appreciation for the arts and academia would not have been seen as particularly masculine in that era, and his parents apparently felt he was in need of some hard labor to toughen him up, so to speak. At the age of eleven, Wright's parents sent him to work on a farm belonging to his mother's brother James (who, when the boy arrived, commented that "[he] had as much muscle as a blackbird's got in his leg"). While Wright would later look back at this time in his life with fondness, crediting it with the development of his rigorous work ethic, at the time, he despised the work. In his Autobiography, he described rising at 4am, dressing in clothes that were as clumsy as they were uncomfortable, then laboring until he fell into bed at half-past seven in the evenings. Throughout the day, he stole as many moments as he could, cutting through woods and meadows. Inevitably, he came to know the land and associate it with the restful solitude he craved while he "piled tired on tired," which is how he would describe his work routine on the farm. Later in his career, he would demand the same piling of "tired on tired" of himself and of his apprentices.

Of his time absorbing the Wisconsin farm's natural beauty, Wright wrote in his Autobiography (in which he wrote of himself in the third person): "He was studying unconsciously what later he would have called 'style'... the boy was some day to learn that the secret of all the human styles in architecture was the same that gave character to trees."

Emerson himself believed that a connection with the divine could only be achieved in solitary communion with nature (this was the same assertion that inspired Henry David Thoreau to seclude himself in the forest and write Walden). Wright's mother, Anna, purchased books by the era's most respected intellectual reformers, such as William Ellery Channing, Theodore Parker, and Thoreau, but it was Emerson who really made an impact on young Wright.

Emerson is now considered the patron saint of Romanticism, a literary and artistic movement that emphasized a oneness with nature (this movement would also influence 19th Century social reforms). His influence is apparent in Wright's architectural style; while the architect is known as the founder of the Prairie Style, he would refer to his aesthetic as Organic Style, the foundation of which is that a building should develop from its natural environment.

6. Originality of style did not gain him recognition until the end of his life

Not the kind of recognition he receives now, anyway. Though currently one of the best-known American architects, Frank Lloyd Wright's style was so modern and his designs considered so outrageous that much of his work was not appreciated until he was an old man – about 90.

Many of his projects inspired vocal opposition, in fact. The first of his structures to cause a ruckus was a windmill he built for his aunts' school. Built in 1896, he called the structure Romeo and Juliet for its double tower (one acting as the prow, the other as an observation tower). His uncles hated it and constantly predicted its collapse, though it survived them all to be renovated in 1989, and is still standing today.

Throughout his career, Wright's houses were thought to be so peculiar that more conventional suburban neighbors referred to them as "harems." In 1928, the Wisconsin State Journal noted that Wright's work "is probably better known in Europe and the Orient than it is in this country." Very few of his structures were held in the same artistic regard as they are today, one exception being his most famous private home, Fallingwater. Shortly after its completion, Fallingwater was featured on January 1938 cover of Time Magazine and is currently registered as a National Historic Landmark (in 2000, it was voted the Building of the Century by the American Institute of Architects). The home was commissioned as a mountain retreat by Edgar J. Kaufmann of Kaufmann's department store fame; it embodies Wright's philosophy of "organic architecture" by blending with its environment, straddling a waterfall in such a way that it appears not to touch solid ground.

When Frederick C. Robie described the type of home he wanted built for himself, an architect he spoke with shouted at him, "You want one of those damn Wright houses!"

Robie, a bicycle manufacturer, responded by hiring Wright to build the now famous Robie House in Chicago, which is on the National Register of Historic Places. The Chicago Theological Seminary, which bought the Robie House in 1926, slated it for demolition twice while Wright was still alive – once in 1941 and again in 1957 – to make way for a dormitory. The house finally earned status as an historic landmark in 1971 and is now considered a prime example of the architect's revolutionary style.

Wright's designs placed value on intimacy of the domestic space, bringing ceilings and doorways down to be slightly higher than human height (in opposition to Victorian-style homes, where spaciousness was valued). He did not want the walls to be thought of "as the side of a box" – rather, they were screens. The living areas were designed to be open, flowing naturally into each other and crossing functions.

In 1969, critic and historian Ryner Banham would call Wright "America's greatest architect to date and the world's best domestic architect since Andrea Palladio [1508–1580 AD]." Wright had been dead for ten years at this point.

7. He was a die-hard momma's boy

In what may be an apocryphal story, Wright's mother, Anna, claimed to know from his conception that he was destined to become a great architect. She cultivated his architectural talents from infancy, decorating his nursery with framed photographs of famous buildings, mainly cathedrals.

On a trip to the Philadelphia Centennial Exposition in 1876, Anna purchased a set of Froebel Blocks for her beloved son. Throughout his life, Wright would speak of the brightly colored wooden blocks as the inspiration for his interest in architecture. The blocks were developed by Friedrich Froebel, a renowned German educator who was instrumental in popularizing the advanced kindergarten method of education to the United States. Froebel was a crystallographer before becoming an educator, and the forms of this science are apparent in his toys and, later, in Wright's own work; "[H]is use of the rotated plan, the flipped mirror image, the hexagonal module, buildings designed in series as typical crystal chains," writes biographer Ada Louise Huxtable.

While Anna was invested in her son's success, her dedication extended beyond his education and intellectual development. Anna favored her son above the other children in his childhood household, especially William's children from his first marriage. Again, this was possibly one cause of strain in William and Anna's marriage, others being financial troubles stemming from William's inability to find lucrative employment (as a Baptist minister, he usually worked for parishes too poor to offer him a living wage).

Perhaps it was this level of investment that inspired Anna to remain at her son's side throughout her life. She wrote to him weekly when he lived in Chicago, and when he made enough money to send for her, he looked for homes further from Lake Michigan because, though he favored the lakefront, Anna disliked it, citing the cold.

Anna vocally protested Wright's marriage to his first wife, Catherine, with whom he would have six children. When the newly married Wright bought a home in Oak Park, Illinois, he made sure there was a cottage for his mother. Later, when he built his home and studio in Wisconsin, one of the first buildings he began work on was a separate home for Anna (located in the valley where she used to send him every summer as a child to work for her brother). Thus, it seemed to be by design on both their parts that Anna was a constant fixture in Wright's life until her own death in 1923.

8. He never saw an electric light bulb until he moved to Chicago as a young man

Because Wright's designs are still looked on as so very forward and modern, it is natural to think of the architect himself as being of the modern era of electricity, telecommunications, and wireless. As an adult, he cut the figure of a worldly sophisticate, but when he first arrived in Chicago, having been born and mainly raised in rural Wisconsin, he had never seen an electric light bulb in person.

Chicago was still in the process of being rebuilt following the Great Fire of 1871 and the recession that followed when Wright arrived on a rainy evening in 1887. He had seven dollars in his pocket, 70 cents of which he immediately spent on something to eat. He then wandered around the city for most of the night, dazzled by the electric lights (he'd never seen a single one, and now he was in a city where thousands of them hummed away in clusters). He rode the cable car, and when he reached the newly constructed Chicago Opera House, he paid another dollar of his reserves to go inside, where it was warm and dry, to listen to a performance.

Chicago would be the center of the architectural world in the coming decades. In six years, the city would be home to the Colombian Exposition, also known as the 1893 World's Fair, one of the largest events on the planet of that year. The fair would be called the White City by fair-goers for its massive light display and classic, crystalline buildings. It was an exciting time for Wright to begin his career in a place where experimental architecture and modern technology blossomed side-by-side.

Wright spent the next few days looking for work, visiting all the architectural firms in the city. His final stop was the firm of Joseph Lyman Silsbee, a popular and highly-respected designer who was also building Wright's Uncle Jenkin's All Souls Church. Whether or not Wright mentioned this coincidence is unknown, but he was hired as a tracer at eight dollars a week. He would, over the next few years, work at a number of well known firms under a number of still famous architects who were well respected in their time. From Silsbee, he went to Beers, Clay and Dutton, back to Silsbee, and finally to Adler and Sullivan, where he found a mentor and role model in co-founder Louis Sullivan.

Sullivan would guide Wright in his quest for a new architecture (for which Sullivan also searched) to accommodate the changes in contemporary American life. In time, Sullivan would become almost a father figure to Wright.

9. He had a second career as a Japanese art dealer

Toward the end of the nineteenth century, the Japanese aesthetic, known as Japonisme, became wildly popular throughout the Western world. Wright himself developed a fascination with Japanese art and culture, especially woodblock prints. So enamored was he with this aesthetic, that he made a second career for himself as a Japanese art dealer. His collection was both a lifelong love affair and an essential source of income; prints sold to the Metropolitan Museum of Art in New York by one F. L. Wright were discovered by historian Julia Meech toward the end of the 20th Century. Meech wrote of this discovery and others in her book, Frank Lloyd Wright and the Art of Japan: The Architect's Other Passion, including Wright's retirement from art dealing when he was deceived in 1919 by a Tokyo dealer who sold him several forged and retouched prints. Wright unwittingly sold these forgeries to some of his best customers, tainting his reputation as an art dealer. Following this unfortunate turn of events, Wright gave up dealing artwork, retaining future purchases solely for his personal collection.

Japanese art and architecture would continue to influence his work throughout his career. His introduction to Japanese architecture came from the Japanese pavilion at the 1893 Columbian Exposition. In addition to an influence on his style, Wright's interest in Japanese culture led to career opportunities; he became the first and only Westerner to design Tokyo's Imperial Hotel, which, due to natural disaster and post-WWII decay, has existed in three different incarnations.

The first Imperial Hotel was destroyed by fire in 1919 (luckily, the owners had already commissioned Wright as an architect to accommodate the hotel's growing number of visitors and improve the outdated design). While the design drew heavily from the style of Wright's own apprentice, Arata Endo, it also, funnily enough, was influenced by Maya Revival Style, which itself draws influence from ancient Mesoamerica.

Additionally, Wright designed the hotel to be earthquake-proof, and while it did survive the Great Quake of 1923, the building was all but destroyed in WWII. As Japan struggled to rebuild in the aftermath of the war, the hotel was neglected and fell into ruin. Having since been rebuilt, the hotel is now in its third incarnation.

His work on the hotel catapulted Wright-san (as he took to calling himself during the construction) to worldwide fame.

10. In the tradition of great artists, Wright courted his own scandal

In one of his most famous statements, Wright asserted that in the struggle between "honest arrogance and hypocritical humility," he would always choose the former. As such, he strove to remain unapologetic, accepting his strengths and his flaws wholeheartedly.

For example, he pointed out in his own Autobiography that he never fully assumed the role of father to the six children he had with his wife, Catherine. He would write that his work was his life, that his designs were his children: "The architect absorbed the father."

While this admission of familial shortcoming is admirable, his philosophy could not be without its inevitable and sometimes catastrophic drawbacks.

One instance that had a particularly negative impact on his career and social life was Wright's choice to leave Catherine when he fell in love with Martha "Mamah" Borthwick Cheney.

Mamah was a friend of Catherine's and wife to Edwin Cheney. She was a highly intelligent, well-read feminist with whom Wright may have become infatuated when he built a home for the Cheneys five years earlier. Meanwhile, Catherine's attention was monopolized by the care of her children and the family's home; she lacked both the time and apparently the inclination for intellectual pursuits. The differences between the two women are striking due to what happened next: in 1909, Wright abandoned his studio and his projects (some of which were completed by his contemporary Marion Mahoney, one of the first female graduates of MIT's architecture program and an artist who was able mimic his style commendably) and left for Europe, accompanied by Mamah. He would later write in his Autobiography: "Because I did not know what I wanted, I wanted to go away."

Some scholars have argued that this was a midlife crisis of sorts for Wright, though he and Mamah remained a couple until her death in 1914. Oddly enough, Catherine refused to grant Wright a divorce until 1922.

11. When Wright first built his home and studio in Wisconsin, nearby homeowners disapproved of their new neighbor

The name Taliesin means "shining brow," and the 6th century Welsh poet of the same name is often called the "Chief of Bards," believed to have sung at the courts of three Celtic kings.

Wright likely chose this name due to his maternal family's Welsh heritage, as well as the fact that the home was built on the "brow" of one of his favorite hills going back to childhood. In accordance with Wright's principles of organic architecture, Taliesin appeared to rise out of the hill's brow; "... not on the land, but of the land," as Wright would say in his Autobiography.

Taliesin is located in Wisconsin's Iowa County near the town of Spring Green. Some of Wright's most famous works were designed at his studio there, including Fallingwater, the Guggenheim Museum, and the first Usonian home (the name Wright used for his middle-income family homes; the name is derived from the Esperanto word for United States, Usono). Shortly after his return from Europe with Mamah, Wright decided to build the home in a valley that had been his family's land since the Civil War.

Aside from providing him with a home and studio, Taliesin would serve an experimental purpose of sorts. Wright used design and materials with which he had little experience. Additionally, Taliesin would have to be rebuilt twice, each time due to fire; the second was apparently caused by a power surge due to a lightening storm, as the fire appeared to have started near a telephone in Wright's bedroom. Each rebuilding resulted in alterations of design and materials, as well as in name (Taliesin subsequently became known as Taliesin II and, later, Taliesin III).

Though Wright had made a name for himself in the region as a talented architect, his neighbors were unenthusiastic to have such a well-known name nearby. Some voiced their disapproval of his separation from his wife and apparently feared he would bring scandal to the area. Their fears are ironic in hindsight, considering that his home is now a major tourist attraction, bringing thousands of admirers of his art to that little corner of rural Wisconsin for decades (and likely for decades to come).

12. Taliesin was the site of one of the most brutal murders in Wisconsin history

As it happened, an event at Wright's Wisconsin home did end up directing national attention on the community, though not in the way his neighbor's expected or feared.

Construction on the home near Spring Green, Wisconsin began in 1911 when Wright returned from Europe with Mamah, who, upon obtaining a divorce from Edwin, now went by her maiden name of Borthwick. When the home, was completed, Mamah moved in along with her own two children. She would spend the rest of her life there.

Wright continued to work mainly out of Chicago, which was where he was when tragedy struck on August 15, 1914.

While Wright oversaw work in Midway Gardens, Julian Carlton, a domestic worker from Barbados whom Wright had hired to work in Taliesin, committed one of the most atrocious massacres Wisconsin had ever seen. Carlton had been in Wright's employ for several months when he bolted the doors and windows on the dining room in Taliesin where six people were eating.

Carlton then set fire to the home, attacking anyone who attempted to escape through the windows with an axe.

While many neighbors rushed to help, most of the victims did not survive. Mamah was killed, along with her two children, Martha and John, handyman David Lindblom, draftsman Emile Brodelle, Taliesin foreman Thomas Brunker, and Ernest Weston, the 13-year-old son of one of Wright's carpenters.

The would-be rescuers quickly raised a posse to search for Carlton, who was found hiding near the scene. Though he was nearly lynched on the spot by the infuriated crowd, the local sheriff managed to get him to the Dodgeville jail – pursued by three cars full of angry neighbors wielding guns.

Carlton would never see trial; he died weeks later due to self-starvation. A motive was never discovered. Not even Carlton's wife, Gertrude, who escaped the fire through a basement window, could shed light on the reason for her husband's actions.

Wright hurried to Taliesin as soon as he heard of the murders, bringing with him Mamah's first husband, Edwin, who was also the father of her two children. After burying Mamah at Unity Chapel, which Wright himself had helped design for his relative Jenkin Lloyd Jones, he wrote an open letter to the community's newspaper, thanking them for their assistance and support, and pledging to rebuild Taliesin in Mamah's memory, which he did, calling the home Taliesin II (not to be confused with Taliesin West in Scottsdale, AZ, which was Wright's winter home upon which he began construction in 1937).

13. He was considered a social reform artist, even designing his own urban utopia

In the nineteenth century, art was often considered a means of facilitating social change. As a child of the nineteenth century, Wright naturally married social and aesthetic progress in his own work. In his later years, contemporary scholars sought him out as a sort of guru of modern social thought. Many of his buildings were designed with the idea of improving life for the average American.

Though Wright himself had a taste for extravagant living (likely due to a childhood of going without, and a habit that would wreck havoc on his finances), his Usonian homes were specifically designed so that the typical middle class American family could afford them. The houses were usually built in a one-story L-shape, with no basement or attic. In the late-1940s, as the country worked to solve the post-war housing shortage, this home design became wildly popular, and houses built in this fashion were marketed as ranch-style homes.

Critics and historians alike would note that his elimination of attics and dormers, including separate servants' quarters, was in itself an act of social reform. His ideals of inclusion and social equality are a recurring theme in his art and his life; he adapted the famous adage regurgitated by designers and laymen alike, "form follows function," and stated that "form and function are one." It harkens back to the transcendentalists, those thinkers who inspired him and who said that art is not just a part of life or a reflection of life, art is life and vice versa.

His philosophies would attract the attention of artists and reformers alike. In 1932, he invited 23 apprentice architects into his home and studio. It was the inaugural year of the Taliesin Fellowship, a school of architecture where Wright's students would "learn by doing," much as he had.

In 1942–43, David Henken apprenticed under Wright. Henken's wife, Priscilla, traveled with him and kept a diary during the year she and her husband spent with the famous architect. Prior to moving to Wisconsin, Priscilla and David lived and raised their three children in a cooperative community they helped found in New York. Their interest in Wright's architecture spawned from their desire to develop their knowledge of urban planning (Wright built a large model city, which he called

Broadacre City, and which showcased his vision of an urban utopia; the model toured the country in 1935). At this point, Wright also had years of experience in community planning, including suburban as well as urban.

Priscilla's diary, which would remain unpublished for 70 years, painted Taliesin as a veritable artists' commune, including cooperative farming, heated political debates, and insights on popular culture. Above all, the Fellows were concerned with how they could use their talents to improve lives and instigate social and economic reform.

14. A twist of fate brought Wright and Taliesin to the forefront of the 1940s draft debate, even landing the architect on an FBI watch list

Wright was a longstanding pacifist, vocally and, as always, unapologetically opposed to violence and war. While this seems like a position with which one could not easily find fault, after the Japanese army attacked Pearl Harbor in 1941, the average American had little patience for passivism.

In the 1940s, a man between the ages of 18 and 65 was required by law to register for Selective Service. A man could register as a conscientious objector; Congress only provided exemptions for Americans to were opposed to war on religious grounds, however, and did not approve those who objected due to moral, philosophical, and/or political grounds.

In WWII, an opposition to war was a popular position among the fellows (though it was in no way an "official" position; nineteen members of the Fellowship were drafted into the armed forces throughout the war). David Henken himself applied for conscientious objector status while in New York, prior to arriving in Wisconsin with his wife, and proudly announced his decision upon arriving at Taliesin.

Another Taliesin apprentice, Marcus Weston, became a national figure, eventually going to prison for his unwillingness to participate in the war. His trial gained the attention of the press as well as the Federal Bureau of Investigation in Washington, D. C. When the Taliesin collective's general attitude toward war was revealed, along with Wright's own antiwar beliefs, the Fellowship drew national attention. Wright himself became the subject of an FBI investigation.

Federal judge Patrick T. Stone went so far as to say, "I think you boys [referring to the Fellows] are living under a bad influence with that man Wright... I'm afraid he is poisoning your minds." In response, Wright wrote an open letter, which was published in newspapers across the country, publicly stating his support of conscientious objection. The letter included a charge against Judge Stone of "using the bench to sound off his prejudice against another man on mere hearsay... [a]s for conscription, I think it has deprived the young men in America of the honor and the privilege of dedicating themselves as freemen to the service of their country.

Were I born forty years later than 1869, I, too, would be a conscientious objector."

15. Though he lived and worked primarily in Chicago, the largest concentration of FLW structures in the world is in Lakeland, FL

In 1938, the same year Fallingwater appeared on the cover of Time magazine, Wright broke ground for the first of a series of buildings on Florida Southern College's campus in Lakeland, Florida. Today, these buildings make up the largest collection of Frank Lloyd Wright buildings in the world, constructed at what is often considered the peak of his career; Wright was 71 years old.

Two years earlier, in 1936, FSC president Ludd M. Spivey paid Wright a visit at his Wisconsin home. A drop in university attendance caused by the Great Depression likely had sway over Spivey's visit, and his inspiration to visit Wright probably came from the architect's longtime criticism of college campuses as "architectural failures." Spivey envisioned a "college of tomorrow," and Wright's design does in fact look like a futuristic vision of Spanish and Eastern European influence.

Collectively, the buildings are called the Florida Southern College Architectural District, or Child of the Sun. The first building was the Annie Pfeiffer Chapel, which, in the tradition of much of Wright's work, was both hailed and reviled upon its completion (Pfeiffer was heard to remark at the dedication ceremony, "they say it's finished," and the building is often referred to as "the bicycle rack" due to the many metal bars incorporated in its design).

Possibly the most futuristic-looking of all the buildings is the Thad Buckner Building, which has a semi-circular, almost disk-like (or flying saucer-like) terrace. Originally the college's library, the building is now home to the Frank Lloyd Wright Visitor Center and Esplanade Gift Shop.

In total, Child of the Sun contains eight buildings as well as the esplanades, and the site is listed in the National Register of Historic Places.

16. The only skyscraper he ever built is located in Bartlesville, Oklahoma

Though Wright designed many skyscrapers throughout his career, only one of them was ever built. The Price Tower in downtown Bartlesville, Oklahoma was constructed in 1956, when Wright was 89 years old, just three years before his death.

The tower is named for Oklahoma businessman Harold Price, who approached Wright to build a three-story headquarters for his pipeline company. Wright countered with a suggestion of 10 stories. According to Price: "We finally compromised on 19 floors."

Additionally, Price's original budget was $750,000, and in the end it would cost $2.1 million. Thus, it was a typical Wright contract. From the beginning of his career to the end, he would always go larger than the client's initial intention (which may be a contributing factor to his status as one of the world's greatest architects).

Called "one of his most bizarre buildings ever" by The Atlantic in 2008, the architect referred to the building as "the tree that escaped the crowded forest." This is partially due to the design's similarity to a pine tree; the building's 19 floors are projected outward from a strong central core, much like tree branches. The "leaves" are the outer walls, which hang from the floors. That the tower "escaped from the crowded forest" is a reference to its design's origins. In the 1920s, a similarly designed apartment complex for St. Marks-in-the-Bowerie was slated to go up in Manhattan, New York City. The Great Depression obliterated finances for the complex, which was then shelved for thirty years until Wright adapted the design for the Price Tower, thus, plucking his "tree," so to speak, from the "crowded forest" of New York City's skyscrapers and depositing it in the midst of the Oklahoma prairie.

The Price Tower currently houses an arts center founded in 1985. The center's focus is mostly art as it relates to architecture and design, containing significant works by Wright himself. The Tower is currently a National Historic Landmark and, along with nine other properties designed by Wright, is listed to become a World Heritage Site.

17. It took him 15 years to design the Guggenheim, which he originally wanted to call the Archseum.

The Solomon R. Guggenheim Museum, often referred to simply as "The Guggenheim," his one of Wright's most famous buildings. It would also be one of his last; his involvement in the project began in 1943, when he was first contacted to design a building that would house Guggenheim's four-year-old Museum of Non-Objective Painting, but Wright would die a little more than six months before the grand opening on October 21, 1959. The world-famous art museum was the first of an international series of museums to be built by the Solomon R. Guggenheim Foundation, a nonprofit organization founded by the businessman and philanthropist whose name it bears.

"Archseum" means "to see from the highest." Wright likely wanted the name because the initial designs included a glass elevator. He produced over 700 sketches for the work, which included other innovative ideas like a vacuum system in the lobby so visitors would not track in dirt (this system, however, was deemed too noisy and the idea was scrapped).

The museum is cylindrical in shape, flaring at the top floors, like an inverted ziggurat. It contains a spiraling, ramped gallery, with all the rooms interconnected. Wright conceived it to be a "temple of the spirit," of which he likely felt New York City was in desperate need. Wright called the city overpopulated and overbuilt, lacking in architectural integrity. It must have been a great relief to him that the museum was to be located across from Central Park, what he likely considered to be the last glimpse of nature within the city.

The architect wanted the museum to be place of respite from the modern world, where people could commune with art and nature amid a metropolis. At one point, he designed a tower that included artists' apartments and studios. The museum's official web site notes that 'Some people, especially artists, criticized Wright for creating a museum environment that might overpower the art inside. "On the contrary," he wrote, "it was to make the building and the painting an uninterrupted, beautiful symphony such as never existed in the World of Art before.' His sentiments have been echoed in museum designs ever since, with architects seeking to create structures that are as artistically worthy as the great works they house.

18. His son John Lloyd Wright is best known for inventing Lincoln Logs

Inducted into the National Toy Hall of Fame in 1999, Lincoln Logs are world famous and commonly considered a childhood staple.

John followed in his father's footsteps, both by becoming an architect and by adopting his father's principles of organic architecture. Like his brother Lloyd, John would apprentice with his father, accompanying him to Tokyo to work in the Imperial Hotel's second incarnation. For sixteen months, John would work with his father, testing the earthquake-proof foundations of the hotel and sketching some of the private commissions the elder Wright had begun to receive from Japanese clients.

John was not the only one of Wright's descendants to follow in his footsteps. His own daughter, Elizabeth Wright Ingraham, became an architect, currently working out of Colorado Springs. Frank Lloyd Wright, Jr., more often known as Lloyd Wright, was a respected architect in the Los Angeles area, and his son Eric Lloyd Wright (Wright's grandson) is currently an architect and owns his own firm in Los Angeles. Other notable descendants include granddaughter Anne Baxter, an Academy Award–winning American actress (The Magnificent Ambersons, All About Eve).

Incidentally, when Wright's stepdaughter, Svetlana (her mother was Wright's third wife, Olga Ivanova Lloyd Wright, with whom he remained until his death in 1959), passed away in 1946, she left behind a widower, William Wesley Peters. In 1970, Peters would marry another Svetlana – Svetlana Alliluyeva, the youngest child and only daughter of Joseph Stalin. While this marriage occurred following Wright's death, it is amusing to imagine how it might have ruffled some feathers among the FBI agents in charge of his surveillance following the conscientious objector debacle.

19. Music was a constant presence in his life

Whatever Wright's feelings about his father, the man left an impression on the architect in the form of a lifelong love of music, which Wright acknowledged.

William Wright, shared his love of music with his children, as well, imparting in them an appreciation for classical musicians such as Johann Sebastian Bach (ostensibly his favorite). As a minister, William rather logically kept an organ in the family home, and Wright often told a story of how his father had him pump the organ for long periods, at times to the point of exhaustion, while William played on, lost in his own world of music.

A keyboard of some kind, usually a piano, was one of the few constants throughout Wright's childhood, and it was one that he kept throughout his life. While constructing the Imperial Hotel in Tokyo, he was able to locate a piano for his living quarters, in spite of such an instrument being rare in post-World War I Japan. There was piano in his winter home, Taliesin West, in Arizona, and even one in his suite at the Plaza Hotel while he oversaw the construction of the Guggenheim.

In her diaries, Priscilla J. Henken mentions music as a constant presence at Taliesin during her husband's turn in the Fellowship. In addition to the always-present piano, Fellows brought in their own instruments, including acoustic guitars, and music was as much a part of daily life at Taliesin as food (which was celebrated) and film (Wright had a special theater built on the farm that showed films on a regular basis – after screenings, there was often discussion amongst the attendants).

Wright was a man who approached all of his projects with such fervor that it left little room for hobbies, in the traditional sense. While he had a wide appreciation of the arts outside of architecture, including literature, film, and photography, music can be considered one of his few, true "hobbies." Throughout his life, he would enjoy making music for its own sake.

20. He had an obsessive work ethic

Though the world is filled with contradicting stories about Wright, his claim to an impassioned work ethic is undisputed. He would often credit his childhood spent working on his Uncle James' farm with developing in him the ability to "pile tired on tired," to work until his energy was gone and then keep working anyway. Alumni of his Fellowship attest that he encouraged them to cultivate similar working habits. Biographers and contemporaries alike have said that he could work longer and harder than men who were far younger, with presumably more vitality, than he.

The extent of his fixation on his work is apparent through his designs for the interiors of his buildings, for he not only designed the structures, but what furniture would go inside, what colors and patterns would make up the decor, and, in the cases of some of his homes, even what dress the hostess would wear while entertaining. Napkins, dining room chairs, and end tables were all to be found among his designs, alongside light fixtures, area rugs, and sofa pillows.

Essentially all of Wright's designs included these interior details. That they are lacking in some of his works, or have had to be reproduced, is due to the fact that some of his interior works were sold off over time by owners. While this is a testament to their standalone artistic merit, the pieces were intended to be viewed as part of a greater whole. Every corner of every room was carefully plotted so that it would look exactly how Wright envisioned it. Thus, his buildings were not just buildings – not in his eyes, anyway. He seemed to think of them as art installations in themselves, even those that were built to house the art of others, such as the Guggenheim. For that museum, Wright designed special chairs and benches on which visitors could pause in their flow from room to room, gallery to gallery, to reflect on the art they viewed and their environment. His furniture was always designed with the idea that it was there to maximize the experience of the space. In order to accomplish this, he had to envision how people would move through the spaces he'd designed, and he would have to anticipate where and when they would make use of his furniture. In considering all of this, it's no wonder he worked as long and as hard as he did; the possibilities are essentially endless.

21. He is arguably the greatest architect in United States history

While choosing the absolute greatest architect in a country's history is beyond problematic, the amount of recognition Wright received following his death (and shortly before) certainly puts him in the running.

One of the most widely acclaimed and awarded architects of the past century, some of his recognitions include several honorary degrees (including one from the University of Wisconsin–Madison), Gold Medal awards from the Royal Institute of British Architects and the American Institute of Architects, and the Franklin Institute's Frank P. Brown Medal. Multiple countries named him an honorary board member to their national academies of art and/or architecture, and the American Institute of Architects has listed him as a Top Ten architect alongside other great American architects such as I. M. Pei, Ludwig Mies van der Rohe, and Eero Saarinen. Several of his buildings are on the United Nations Educational, Scientific, and Cultural Organization (UNESCO) World Heritage Site list, and he has even been featured on a United States Postal Service stamp (in 1966 – it was the 2 cent in the Prominent American series).

Now studied and appreciated by professionals and laymen alike, Wright is indeed a contender for greatest architect in the nation's history. Ever self–assured and unapologetic, however, Wright would insist upon calling himself the undisputed master of architecture in the 20th century. One famous (and perhaps apocryphal) story tells of how he, while testifying in court, was asked by an official to identify himself. Wright responded by declaring that he was the greatest architect in the world. His response, when asked how he could make such a statement, was that he had no choice – he was under oath.

More information can be found about Richland Center and the Frank Lloyd Wright-designed warehouse restoration project by visiting www.HometownWright.com.

Also visit www.FrankLloydWrightStories.com for a series of behind the scenes videos with the author.

BIB:

Curtis, Wayne. "Little Skyscraper on the Prairie." The Atlantic. July/August 2008. 28 Dec. 2012. <http://www.theatlantic.com/magazine/archive/2008/07/little-skyscraper-on-the-prairie/306843/>

Henken, Priscilla J. Taliesin Diary: A Year With Frank Lloyd Wright. New York City, NY: W. W. Norton and Company, Inc., 2012.

Huxtable, Ada Louise. Frank Lloyd Wright: A Life. New York City, NY: Penguin Books, 2004.

National Register of Historic Places, <http://nps.gov>

The Solomon R. Guggenheim Foundation,
<http://www.guggenheim.org>

Wright, Frank Lloyd. Frank Lloyd Wright:
An Autobiography. Pomegranate, 2005.

25225444R00035

Printed in Great Britain
by Amazon